Procrastinate
Less
and
Enjoy Life More

**A procrastinator's guide
to self-improvement**

Other Books by Harold L. Taylor

Making Time Work For You
Personal Organization: The Key to
    Managing Your Time and Your Life
Managing Your Memory
Delegate: The Key to Successful
    Management
Making Time to Sell
Manage Your Meetings
The Educated Executive
Getting Organized
28 Time Problems and How to Solve Them
The Administrator's Guide to Effective
    Time Management
Time Worp: 750 Ways to Save Time
Say Yes to Your Dreams

Procrastinate Less

and
Enjoy Life More

A procrastinator's guide
to self-improvement

HAROLD L. TAYLOR

Author of the bestseller
Making Time Work For You

Published 1999 by Harold Taylor Time Consultants Inc.
2175 Sheppard Ave. E., Suite 310, North York, Ontario,
Canada M2J 1W8. 416-491-0777

Canadian Cataloguing in Publication Data

Taylor, Harold L.
        Procrastinate less and enjoy life more : a procrastinator's
guide to self-improvement

Includes bibliographical references and index.
ISBN 0-9683670-1-1

        1.   Procrastination. 2. Success in business. 1. Title.
BF637.P76T39 1999   650.1   C99-901520-6

To my Mother and Dad: I wanted to dedicate a book to you while you were still alive, but I kept putting it off.

Contents

some things *should* be delayed and other things *must* be delayed. You're not a hardened procrastinator unless the delay is intentional and repetitive. /30

5.   Doing what comes naturally.
Procrastination is a natural response since it's only normal to want to avoid unpleasantness. And the benefits of doing something right away are usually not as immediate as the reward of avoidance. /34

6.   Other reasons we procrastinate.
The desire to avoid distasteful or overwhelming tasks are not the only reasons we procrastinate, although they are the most common ones. Other reasons include the fear of success, fear of failure and perfectionism. /38

7.   The path of least resistance.
Doing what comes naturally is not always the best thing to do. To eliminate procrastination we must fight our natural tendencies. /42

8.   Developing the *do it now* habit.
Procrastination only exists in relationship to a task or activity. It is impossible to eliminate procrastination completely, but we can reduce its occurrences immensely. /46

9.   If it's distasteful, get rid of it.
If you are bothered by distasteful tasks, the best way out is to do it right away and get it over with. Prompt action usually improves the situation as well as your state of mind. **/50**

10.   Overcoming the overwhelming.
Taking bites from huge tasks makes them less overwhelming. Keeping goals in sight makes them more achievable. **/54**

11.   Use the chunk method.
No task is too large if it is tackled a chunk at a time. Successful people do a little at a time, again and again. **/58**

12.   Make commitments, not lists.
A list of things to do provides the temptation to choose the easy ones and provides no commitment to get the important things done. Scheduling is a much more effective process. **/62**

13.   Delaying decisions wastes time & impedes success.
One of the worst things to put off is decision-making. Here are some suggestions for making decisions that should neutralize the tendency to procrastinate. **/66**

14.   Motivation can conquer procrastination.
Generating enthusiasm and concentrating on the rewards of completion instead of the unpleasantness of the activity can raise the motivation to get on with the job /70
.

15.   Get organized.
Disorganization breeds procrastination. By following some proven time management strategies you can reduce the likelihood of chronic delay. /74

16.   Perfectionism is procrastination's ally.
If you wait until you have enough time to do a job right, you may never get it done. When *right* means perfect, you are a procrastinator. /80

17.   Don't be afraid of fear.
Fear and worry, whether unfounded or not, can produce procrastination. But you can reduce fear and worry and act in spite of the fear. /86

18.   Plan to say no.
Without intentionally putting things off, you may have to delay simply because other people's priorities take precedence over your own. You must say no more often. /90

19.   Fight procrastination with routines.
Developing routines can make it easier to work on unpleasant tasks and reduce the tendency to procrastinate. /94

20. Working with procrastinators.
You may not procrastinate yourself, but have to work with people who do. Here are some suggestions for insuring that *others* get things done on time.

21. Twenty-five ways to overcome procrastination.
Here is a summary of the most effective ways of reducing the tendency to procrastinate. Choose those that will help you the most.

Conclusion.
Procrastination is eliminated a little at a time. Don't be discouraged: be persistent

Introduction

I put off writing this book for years. It seemed like an overwhelming task. After all, don't books have to be at least 50,000 words and over 200 pages in length? And the research required! I would have to come up with dozens of case studies, references, and examples. I just didn't have that much time. There were so many other things that I had promised to get done.

It certainly wasn't a very pleasant experience to look forward to. I hated the tedious research that would be necessary and the meticulous steps I would have to go through from the outline stage to the final manuscript. And what did I really know about procrastination anyway? Who am I to write a book on a topic that only psychologists are qualified to tackle?

And what if it were no good? What if it were criticized by reviewers and ridiculed by business associates and friends? One bad book could ruin my reputation as a time management expert. I might not be able to find a publisher for it. And if I published it myself, I'd have to risk a lot of money.

If it *did* sell well, look at the pressure I'd be under to live up to the book's claim. People would expect me to be an authority on procrastination. I might be called upon to lecture to companies, schools and associations. How could I live up to everyone's expectations?

Are you beginning to get the point? None of us are immune to the tendency to procrastinate. We put things off for a variety of reasons. We may see the task as overwhelming or unpleasant. It could be that we are wrestling with perfectionism or a negative attitude. Perhaps we're afraid of failure or even success. It could be we have a low self-image or have become a chronic worrier. Maybe we have a problem saying no, have overextended ourselves or simply aren't organized.

But it doesn't have to be that way. We can change all that. We can gain control of our own lives and shake the procrastination habit. After all, I *did* write this book. And I did it by practicing the principles outlined here. The book's not perfect by a long shot. In fact it's brief, flawed and has little chance of becoming a bestseller. But so what? It's finished. And that's a lot better than having an idea that never sees the light of day. Or feeling guilty because something important is left undone. Or never experiencing the joy of seeing a dream come true.

You too can stop procrastinating, improve your personal productivity and get more out of life. First, you have to read this book. But that's easy, even if you're a chronic procrastinator.

In fact, this book was *written* for procrastinators. There are no 50,000 words here. There are not 200 pages here, nor long drawn out case studies nor filler material. The book is brief, with short chapters, written in simple language. It has large type in a readable font with extra space between the lines. It can be read quickly and easily in short sessions while commuting, waiting in a doctor's office or filling time until a meeting starts. It practices what it preaches. There is no reason to put off reading this book. So go to it. Now.

1 Are you a procrastinator? Join the club

Are you a procrastinator?
Join the club

Procrastinators are not rare. People in my time management seminars have constantly rated procrastination as one of their major time problems. There is even a *Procrastinator's Club of America* that boasts 4000 members. And that doesn't count the half million members who haven't got around to paying their dues yet! An article in the *St. Petersburg Times* announced that Les Waas, elected president in 1956 still holds that office, since the association hasn't held their 1957 elections yet. Another article from a different publication explained the association's difficulty in selecting the *Procrastinator of the Year*. To quote, "The nominating committee never gets around to suggesting any names. They share the belief that if anything is really worth doing, it's worth putting off."

Although operating in a light vein, this Philadelphia-based Club actually exists. I wrote for information, and after a 2 ½ month delay received a reply which opened with, *"Dear Fellow Procrastinator: Please forgive our sending the enclosed application for membership so few weeks after your request, but all of a sudden our work got all caught up and there was nothing else left for us to do."*

Even the *Procrastinator's Club of America* is suffering the effects of procrastination because so many people never get around to joining. The club, whose members believe that anything worth doing is worth putting off - is still in the middle of its 1983 membership drive. The address several years ago was Box 712, Bryn Athyn, PA 19009. It may have changed. If so, I'm sure they'll notify their members in due time. As far as I know, new members still receive a copy of the latest newsletter, published in 1976.

Although many people make jokes about procrastination, it is more than an annoying habit. It can be detrimental to our success, happiness, and in some cases, our very lives.

2 Procrastinators pay their dues

Procrastinators pay their dues

A chronic procrastinator's view of time is distorted. They feel there's plenty of time in the future to work on their goals. Even a two week deadline seems like plenty of time. Why there's days left yet! They don't seem to come to grips with the fact that time is finite. There's only so much time in a day, month, year or lifetime. Some people actually put off living until it's too late. Of all the consequences of procrastination, the worst of all has to be cheating ourselves of the opportunity to experience life fully.

Consequences can be either external, internal or both. External consequences include things such as fines for overdue library books, interest charges on loans, reprimands by the boss or family members, or even the loss of a job. Internal consequences include frustration, anger at yourself, feeling pressured or guilty, becoming self-critical, or never knowing the joy of experiencing something you have dreamed of doing.

I've never seen figures on how much money is lost in this country through procrastination, but it must be in the billions. Check the line-ups at the post office on the last day for tax returns, or the final day for *anything* for that matter. According to one author, an estimated 10 million people in the U.S. buy their Valentine's Day gift or card on

February 14th. How many people buy their Christmas cards a few months before Christmas? Why not? Is it too early? Do they self-destruct if kept more than ten days before mailing?

Sometimes procrastination has minor consequences. At other times, it results in death, injury, or unfulfilled lives. There is even the odd time that procrastination produces *favorable* results (and oh, how we love to rationalize our habit by recalling *those* occasions.) But the habit of procrastination, regardless of the results, is self-defeating in the long run. It makes us feel guilty because we realize it's wrong. It's debilitating because we're constantly dreading the task being postponed. We're more tired mentally by *not* doing something than we would be physically if we were to *do* it.

The activity we are postponing could be unpleasant in itself, such as weeding the garden - if that's an activity that we deem unpleasant. Or its magnitude could be unpleasant. An activity such as writing a book could be overwhelming if we dwell on the length of time it would take. We tend to put off tasks that are either unpleasant for us, such as writing statistical reports, doing the laundry, or reprimanding a staff member - or those that will take an overwhelming length of time, such as saving $5000 for a trip to Europe, finishing a rec room or writing a book.

You can usually spot a chronic procrastinator at work. They have cluttered desks, an overflowing in-basket, stacks of unopened magazines, papers to be filed and a "To Do" list that gets longer every day. You have to continually follow up to get anything from them. They frequently cancel appointments, reschedule meetings, and cancel out of seminars at the last minute. They're usually flustered, disorganized and under constant pressure. And generally have a poor self-image.

3 What's your procrastination quotient?

What's your procrastination quotient?

Are you a chronic procrastinator or simply a casual delay artist? To determine how serious a procrastinator you really are, indicate whether the following statements are true, partly true, or false. In the spaces to the left of each statement enter *2* if true, *1* if partly true, and *0* if false.

___ I feel pressured about all the things I have yet to do.

___ I sometimes put off doing a task until it's either too late or I'm embarrassed to do it.

___ I like to stick with a task until it's perfect.

___ I frequently go back to work with my "homework" still in my briefcase untouched.

___ I frequently tell myself, "I'll put it here for now and put it away later."

___ I sometimes think that by delaying a task long enough it won't have to be done.

___ I intend to do things only to forget about them later.

___ I have at least two major projects at work or at home that I am leaving until I have more time.

___ I tend to leave things until the last minute, such as income tax returns, payment of speeding tickets, Christmas shopping, etc.)

___ My mail tends to pile up on my desk or in-basket.

___I have a stack of magazines waiting to be read or several books I haven't got around to reading yet.

___ I am frequently late or rushed when going to meetings, dinner engagements, church functions, etc.

___ I am usually one of the last ones on the block to take down my Christmas decorations, trim my trees, cut my grass, plant my garden, close up the cottage.

___ There are times each year when I have been unable to book a lodge, flight, theatre or sporting event because I had left it too late.

___ I have several broken items at home waiting to be repaired or articles of clothing waiting to be mended.

_____ Total Points

Add the number of points in the spaces to the left of the statements. If you have more than 10 points, you are prone to procrastination. If you have more than 20 points you probably delayed taking this test. If you have 30 points, it's amazing that you ever got around to reading this book, let alone taking the test! But now that you have *started* reading, don't stop. You're on a roll. By the time you finish this book, you will want to dig right into all those other books that you purchased but haven't got around to reading yet.

4 What is procrastination?

What is procrastination?

Common definitions of procrastination include *putting off until later those things that should be done today* or *putting off high priority activities by doing low priority activities instead.* But these are oversimplifications that make us look worse than we really are. We may not have much of a choice. Perhaps the boss *insists* that we finish the unimportant task first. Or maybe it's only a one-time delay. Or it could be that we simply forgot. Or something unforeseen cropped up that couldn't be ignored.

Don't be too hard on yourself. Procrastination is really *the intentional and habitual postponement of some important task that should be done now.* Any time you make a decision to do something at a specific time in the future, you are not procrastinating, you are planning. But if the postponement is *habitual*, i.e. you put it off until the next day, and then the next day, and then the next, and it's not merely a case of forgetting or being coerced into ignoring it, you're procrastinating. And it's still procrastination regardless of the excuses you have or the rationalizations you make for putting it off.

That's why procrastination is such an insidious time waster. It's deceitful. We make it look as though we don't have time to do it, or that it makes sense to polish off the small tasks first to get them out of the way, or that we're saving time in the event that the boss changes his or her mind, or that the urgency of the unimportant tasks is forcing us to do them first. There seems to be no limit to the excuses that people come up with for putting off something that should be done now.

We realize that the present is all we have - that tomorrow may be too late. We are also aware that putting off today's tasks simply adds to tomorrow's burdens. And none of us wants to be one of those people who spends their whole life preparing to live and never getting around to enjoying each moment as it comes. And yet we procrastinate. Why?

5 Doing what comes naturally

Doing what comes naturally

Some things *have* to be delayed; others *should* be delayed. But if we continually and intentionally put off doing high priority activities by doing low priority activities instead, we are procrastinating. We straighten our desk, sharpen our pencils, empty the wastebasket, instead of writing a position paper on gang violence in the schools. We sweep the sidewalk, putter in the garden, smooth the kinks out of the garden hose instead of taking the kids on an excursion to Wonderland. We thumb through magazines, read the paper, watch TV, instead of getting started on that article we've always wanted to write.

Priorities differ from person to person. A kinkless garden hose may be more important to someone than exercise or recreation or family time. But we all know what our own priorities are. They are those meaningful activities that, when completed, bring a sense of achievement and satisfaction. They are the activities that help us to attain those personal and professional goals and desires that burn within us.

It is amazing how adept we are at thinking of other things to do when facing an important task. You would think that we would be enthusiastic about an activity that would produce gain, satisfaction, and a sense of achievement. Unfortunately the satisfaction is not always immediate. The gain is not always something we can readily perceive. Few things worthwhile come without effort, inconvenience, or discomfort. Our natural tendency is to avoid unpleasantness. So we sacrifice long-term benefits in favor of those minor, short-term rewards.

It's only natural to want to relax after dinner instead of washing dishes, even though the delayed task will be even more difficult after the food stains have been allowed to harden. And who could fault us for leaving the broken stair unrepaired until after the football game, even though it presents a safety hazard? And sleeping in on Sunday morning requires less effort than taking the family to church. There is always a diversion at hand to make shirking our responsibility to others and to ourselves more palatable.

6 Other reasons we procrastinate

Other reasons we procrastinate

Like the definition itself, the reason we procrastinate may be more complicated than it looks. We're certainly not born that way. There is no such thing as a *procrastination gene*. Common reasons suggested in books include perfectionism, fear of success or fear of failure. And I can see how these things could impact us. If we're perfectionists, we could be delaying until we have time to do it *right*. Unfortunately we will rarely have more time in the future than we have in the present. In fact, today's future is tomorrow's present. So the delay becomes chronic. If we fear either success or failure, then certainly not doing something will avoid both.

I used to wonder how anyone could possibly be afraid of being successful until someone in that situation shared his feelings with me. It was partly the fear of what it would mean in terms of lifestyle, relationships, personal integrity, and the pressure to maintain peak performance. I can understand that if our sense of self-worth is tied to our performance, we may feel we have to use our abilities to constantly perform at our peak. If we delay performing, that does not detract from our ability, and we can maintain our self-esteem. And by not performing, we can't fail.

To solve the above problems might require

the help of a psychologist or therapist, or at least a skilled counselor - not a time management expert. I do discuss perfectionism in more detail in chapter 16. Meanwhile my suggestion would be not to equate your value with your performance. You are valuable as a person regardless of whether you succeed or fail. And to take the pressure off yourself, ask "What's the impact on my life or job if I don't do something perfectly? Or if I make a mistake? Or if I perform a certain task poorly?" Chances are the consequences would be minimal. It's not the end of the world. If we are procrastinating for these reasons we are playing mind games with ourselves and perhaps we do need professional help to sort things out.

But I believe that most procrastinators simply view a certain task or activity as being either unpleasant or overwhelming. And in these cases a time management approach would stand a good chance of succeeding.

7 The path of least resistance

The path of least resistance

If you pass dozens of service stations that have no line-ups, yet don't stop for gas even if you're not in a hurry, simply because your gas tank is not quite empty, I'd call that procrastinating. Chances are, when your tank is on empty, you'll be rushing along a highway to meet a client, with not a service station in sight.

Now you can't tell me this involves a fear of failure or fear of success or perfectionism. It involves a resistance to performing even a mildly unpleasant task - in this case stopping and filling up your gas tank. Similarly we put off replying to letters, conducting minor repairs around the house, making cold calls, making an appointment to see a doctor or dentist for the same reason. If we view the task as unpleasant, we'll avoid it as long as we can. We'll procrastinate. Our natural tendency is to take the path of least resistance.

I say *natural* because there's nothing abnormal about our behavior. We need not feel like weirdos simply because we procrastinate. Nor do we have to put ourselves on a guilt trip or be too self-critical. We're just being normal.

But just because we're doing what comes naturally doesn't mean we're doing what is best for ourselves. We can become more effective, more productive and more successful than the *normal* people by developing the *do it now* habit. It's not easy or everyone would do it. If you procrastinate on unpleasant tasks again and again, you eventually form the habit of procrastination. And habits are hard to break. Maxwell Maltz, author of the book, *Psychocybernetics*, suggested it takes 21 days to form a habit, so be prepared to invest a little time and effort. But the payoff will be big!

8 Developing the do it now habit

Developing the do it now habit

To change a bad habit we must first recognize that we have one. Then, to replace it with a good habit, we must act out the new behavior we're trying to acquire - again and again - until it is automatic. Chances are there are several jobs or types of jobs that we tend to put off. Once we have identified them, we must concentrate on them one at a time. We can't tackle all the jobs at once; but we *can* focus our energies on one of them. For example, if you tend to put off filing, make up your mind now that you will spend ten minutes at the end of each day filing the accumulated papers. Initially you will have to muster all the willpower you have to make yourself do that job. But after you have forced yourself to do it for 21 days or more, it will not require the same degree of energy. It will become a habit. And success breeds success. You will find you tackle the next distasteful task with a little more enthusiasm.

This may seem like a long process if you procrastinate on a lot of jobs. And it is. But I don't believe you can eliminate procrastination itself. Procrastination is always linked with a task, activity or goal. We can only eliminate procrastination as it relates to those tasks that we are always delaying. It took a long time for us to develop bad habits, so it makes sense that it would take a long time to replace them with good habits. But the more you succeed, the easier it gets. What you eventually develop is self-discipline. And self-discipline is the key to successful self-management.

9 If it's distasteful, get rid of it

If it's distasteful, get rid of it

We tend to postpone jobs that are unpleasant. If we have to deny a request, cancel an order, work on that boring statistical report, we drag our feet. And why not? It's distasteful. So we worry about it. We get upset. Stressed. Oh, how we dread the time when we cannot postpone it any longer and finally *have* to act. But act we must, and when we finally do — what a relief! A load has been lifted from us.

Why suffer by dragging out the inevitable? Get the *do it now* habit. Don't tell yourself, "It's unpleasant, so I'll delay action." Say instead, "It's unpleasant, so I'll do it now and get it over with." Your effectiveness will increase because an unpleasant task isn't hanging over your head. You won't be under stress. And your prompt action may prevent further complications or embarrassment, squelch rumors, and improve relationships. Replace the procrastination habit with the *do it now* habit.

There are ways to make the process easier. Some people believe that if they make a public announcement or tell a friend about their commitment to stop procrastinating on a certain task, the incentive to persist is increased. Others believe the promise of a reward for succeeding helps. Performing the distasteful task during your prime time - that part of the day when you are more mentally alert and energetic - tends to make it easier. For most people this is first thing in the morning. A related idea is to leave the paperwork or project file on your desk before going home at night, the thought being it will be the first thing your eye lights on in the morning. Or schedule it in your planner at a specific time. The important thing to remember is not to try to wipe out procrastination all at once.

Set realistic goals for yourself. And don't be too hard on yourself. Nobody's perfect.

There's only one cure for procrastination, and you're it! You must decide right now to take control of your own life. Set goals, determine your priorities, schedule your activities, and develop the *do it now* habit. If it's unpleasant, yet must be done, do it now and get it over with. It has been said that if you have to swallow a frog, it doesn't pay to look at it too long! Long, seemingly overwhelming tasks can be worked at a little at a time until it's eventually finished. The secret is to *start*. And to do it *now*!

10 Overcoming the overwhelming

Overcoming the overwhelming

The other major reason we procrastinate on a job or a long-term goal is that we view it as an overwhelming task. We feel it's going to take a long time, and we don't have time right now, so we leave it until later. But we never seem to have the time later either. So we add it to a *to do* list. Unfortunately a *to do* list does nothing to further the progress of a task. In fact, it becomes a procrastination tool in itself. There's no commitment in a *to do* list.

It's difficult to complete a task when there's no end in sight. Swimmer Florence Chadwick was said to have failed in her swim from Catalina Island because she couldn't see the shore. How many tasks have you started but never finished because they were overwhelming? You couldn't see the end. They seemed to go on forever. You became discouraged and eventually quit, telling yourself that you would work on it later.

Many people procrastinate simply because it's too formidable a task or there isn't enough time to do it now. What they don't seem to realize is that they don't have to do it *all* now. They only have to do a little at a time for an extended period of time. For example, no one could eat six gallons of ice cream at one sitting, and yet the average Alaskan is said to easily consume that much over a period of one year.

Similarly, most of the jobs that produce the greatest value take longer periods of time. So they are the ones that encourage procrastination. In order to ensure their completion, we should break the jobs into chunks, providing interim *finish times* so the *ends* are always in sight and we maintain our motivation to complete each segment. If we have to call 100 clients, for instance, interim goals might be to contact ten clients each day for ten days. The achievable and more palatable goal of ten replaces the overwhelming mark of 100.

Don't take on too much at a time. Instead of cleaning out a filing cabinet, tackle one drawer or one file at a time. Instead of writing a book, set a goal of one chapter. Instead of trying to save over $1200 in a year, save $100 each month. The ultimate deadline for the job remains the same, but no segment of it is overwhelming.

11 Use the chunk method

Use the chunk method

Most of us tend to procrastinate if the job is a big one. We kid ourselves into thinking we'll have a larger block of time available at a later date. But we never do. The trick is to start the task regardless of whether we have five minutes or five hours. At least we can bring the task five minutes closer to completion. There's no such thing as an insurmountable task, only long links of small tasks that collectively seem insurmountable.

For example, we never wallpaper a whole room. We paper one strip at a time, one wall at a time, until the whole room is papered. Similarly, we don't write a book. That's an overwhelming task. We simply write a series of paragraphs, which link together to form a chapter, which in turn link with other chapters to form a book. We must approach large tasks this way or we will never get the courage to tackle them at all. We'll procrastinate.

If you want to move three hundred files from your filing cabinet to the office down the hall, simply grab a dozen or so every time you head in that direction. Within a few weeks you will have moved them all. If you have to write something involving a long, involved procedure, simply spend ten minutes each day writing one step of that procedure. If you have to clean out a closet at home, tackle only one hanger or one carton each night.

So if you want to accomplish any goal, whether it be to write a book or take a degree course or simply complete a business project, you must work at it in small chunks - a bit at a time - until it's complete. No task is too large or too overwhelming if you work at it a little at a time. If you don't think it will work, think about the things that you *don't* want to get done, like life itself, for example. I have lived life only a minute at a time, and here I am in my sixties already! And it didn't seem to take very long. Just think, if I could have accomplished just one small task each day of my life, how prolific I would be. I could have written one hundred books instead of a dozen. Who couldn't write a page or two each day? If I had saved a few dollars each day, I'd be in a lot better position to retire. And who can't save a dollar or two each day? Imagine making one extra cold call each day, or developing one new product each month or taking one degree course each decade. *Successful people do a little at a time, again and again.*

So don't think about the project in its entirety, and become discouraged. Think about the small chunk, the short-term goal, the little tasks that collectively become the major project. You move a thousand files to a new location a few files at a time. You wallpaper a room a wall at a time. And you clean the basement or garage one shelf at a time.

12 Make commitments, not lists

Make commitments, not lists

If you start work with a list of ten items to do and stop at night with a list of fifteen, including the original ten, you may be a victim of the *to do* list fallacy. A list of things to do serves as a reminder of all the things not yet done, but provides no commitment to actually do them. In fact, it encourages procrastination since it includes all those other more pleasant, easier tasks that could tempt you away from those that *should* be done now.

Instead of keeping everything together on one list, separate the priority, high-payback activities from the items of lesser importance and schedule these *must do* items directly into your planning calendar along with your meetings and appointments. For example, the development of a needed policy manual should never remain on a *to do* list. Block out the time needed in your planner, let's say between 2:30 p.m. and 4:00 p.m. and treat it as though it were a meeting with the boss. Close your door and have calls intercepted if that's what you would do if it were a meeting with someone else. But allow a little extra time for those unavoidable interruptions that are bound to occur. If you schedule several of these meetings with yourself during the week, you will accomplish those priority jobs, decrease the tendency to procrastinate and increase your effectiveness.

To do lists are fine for grocery shopping; but if you're a results-oriented person, a scheduled commitment is a must. Don't be discouraged if some of your scheduled activities have to be changed. A schedule is a guideline and must be flexible. But resist changing your schedule simply to accommodate tasks of no greater importance than your originally planned activity. If a salesperson shows up unexpectedly, for instance, don't abandon your priorities in favor of an impromptu meeting. Block off periods of time in your planning calendar with the intent of following through with them. But don't stop scheduling even if your plans have to be frequently altered. Doctors don't stop scheduling office appointments simply because they are frequently called out on emergencies.

The first thing you schedule into your planner should be blocks of time to work on your goal-related activities. This will ensure that you are working on the 20 percent of the activities that will produce 80 percent of your results, thus avoiding the opportunity to procrastinate.

I designed the *Taylor Planner* with a goals page near the front. Here one could list those priority projects which they want to accomplish during the year. If you are using a different planner, you might consider inserting a similar page. Don't include the routine jobs or those obligations that do little to further your company's or your personal goals.

Include the important things that you have been putting off year after year simply because you haven't had the time to work on them. These goals could be personal as well as professional and might include such things as the writing of a book, the redecorating of a home, or planning a trip to Europe.

In order to determine the target date (recorded in the column to the right of the goal,) estimate how many hours it would take to complete the task. In some cases, this is impossible to determine accurately. If so, simply guess, then add up to 50% to be on the safe side. For example, if you feel it could take 100 hours of solid writing to finish a book, make it 150 hours. Then divide this figure by the number of weeks you plan to work that year. For example, if you work 50 weeks, then the number of hours each week that you will have to work on your goal-related activity should be three. Since it is difficult to work steadily for three hours on any activity, break this into two sessions of one-and-a-half hours each. To accomplish your goal of writing a book, you would have to spend one and-a-half hours twice per week in order to complete it by the end of the year. If this amount of time is unrealistic, set the goal for the end of the following year and work half as long each week. Don't be impatient; be realistic.

13 Delaying decisions wastes time and impedes success

Delaying decisions wastes time and impedes success

Slow decision-making wastes time, as do spur-of-the-moment decisions that result in costly and time-consuming mistakes. But the worst thing you can do is procrastinate on decision-making. Napoleon Hill once conducted a survey of successful people and found all of them were decisive. Don't be afraid of being wrong. We learn from our mistakes; but if we do nothing we neither accomplish anything nor learn anything. Here are a few decision-making tips to keep in mind:

➤ Delay until you have enough information, but don't wait until you have *all* the information. If you have all the information, the course of action becomes a foregone conclusion; no real decision is necessary. Have the courage to make decisions with only 70 to 80 percent of the facts. Otherwise, you're procrastinating. Too many people involved in the decision-making process slow it down considerably. Invite only those people whose views are critical to the situation. Important decision-making sessions should not be used as morale-boosting participation sessions, with everyone having a say. There are other less costly ways of getting involvement.

➤ Delegation improves decision-making since

those people on the front lines make decisions more effectively on a daily basis. Train the people who report to you, delegate authority, and trust them to decide. But be careful what you delegate. There are some decisions that can only be made at your level.

➤ Spend time in proportion to the importance of the decision. Don't waste a lot of time discussing the menu for the staff Christmas party. A decision to close down an operation or expand a product line warrants a greater expenditure of that costly commodity called time. Make minor decisions quickly. If the consequence of the decision is not important, it is not worth much of your valuable time.

➤ When decisions require problem-solving tactics, hold a brainstorming session with your key people. The process could yield fresh ideas, which would not have surfaced otherwise.

➤ If the decision is yours alone to make, and you seem to be bogged down in the process, getting frustrated by your lack of progress, it's frequently faster in the long run to leave the problem for a while. Work on some unrelated jobs for a few hours or even a few days, then tackle the problem anew. The change in pace will revitalize your thinking. But don't do this repeatedly or its procrastination.

➤ Always make short-term decisions with long

range objectives in mind. Don't make a *Band-Aid* decision that solves the immediate problem but results in time-consuming problems further down the road.

➢ Don't waste time on past decisions. Instead of saying, "If only I had," say, "Next time I will."

14 Motivation can conquer procrastination

Motivation can conquer procrastination

It's difficult to accomplish great things in life, since many of those *things* seem overwhelming. But as we have already noted, by breaking tasks down into manageable parts or steps, our goals are not so overwhelming. Michel Lotito of Grenoble, France had a goal to eat a bicycle. But he didn't toss it onto the kitchen table and eat it all at once. He melted it into small swallowable portions and consumed it bit by bit over a period of time.

Eating a bicycle would not be viewed as a great achievement to most people, but the point is that almost anything can be accomplished if we work at it a little at a time. However, we must have the *motivation* to keep at it. No doubt Mr. Lotito had to face some very unpleasant lunches in order to accomplish his feat. And he probably would not have gotten past the handlebars if he had not reminded himself of his goal to get into the *Guinness Book of World Records.*

We tend to procrastinate on distasteful tasks because we lack motivation. Yet if we visualized a task as a stepping-stone to a goal we greatly desired, motivation would increase. For example, few people enjoy jumping out of bed at 5 a.m. to face a routine day. But if getting up at 5 a.m. ensured that we connected with the 7 a.m. departure of a plane headed for Hawaii, the chore of rising early is seen in an entirely different light. Similarly, a boring subject at school is not as distasteful when viewed as a stepping-stone to graduation. Exercise is more palatable when viewed as a way of remaining healthy. And making cold calls on prospects is not as unpleasant when it's done to win a sales award, exceed our quota, earn a promotion or achieve some other desirable goal.

The point here is that we should set goals for ourselves and view each task, pleasant or otherwise, as stepping stones in the achievement of those goals. Our thoughts should not dwell on the unpleasantness or difficulty of the task, but on the joy of achieving the goal.

If unpleasant tasks do not help to achieve a personal or organizational goal, perhaps they *should* be delayed, or avoided altogether. Only the important tasks merit our attention. And the important tasks are those that will help us achieve our goals.

Procrastination is a case of mind over matter. If the job doesn't matter to us, we let it slip from our mind. Make it matter by constantly reviewing the benefits of achieving the overall goal. Motivation goes a long way to helping us overcome the tendency to procrastinate.

To overcome the habit of procrastination, we must generate some enthusiasm to offset the unpleasantness. We must concentrate, not on the activity, but on the reward awaiting us upon completion. If the activity is unpleasant, let us pounce on it immediately and complete it so we won't have to dwell on its unpleasantness. If it's an overwhelming activity, let us chop it up into manageable chunks and polish it off a piece at a time. If we have to drive across the country, let's aim at driving six hours each day. If we have to write a book, let's aim at completing ten typewritten pages each day. If we have to pack the contents of a house in preparation for moving, let's aim at packing two cartons each day.

Motivation is the product of our desire to achieve a goal and the expectancy that we will be successful in achieving it. Even though we may want something badly, if we don't feel we have a chance of achieving it, our motivation will be low. Keep your motivation high by raising your expectation of achieving each goal.

Author Ari Kiev once wrote, *"When you postpone your involvement in something, you will probably never accomplish it, and will be left with memories of past wishes rather than past deeds."* Yesterday will never come again, and tomorrow may never arrive; but today is ours. Let's make the most of it.

15 Get organized

Get organized

Although reluctance to start unpleasant or time-consuming tasks is the major cause of procrastination, some people are simply disorganized. They lack clear-cut goals, don't plan or schedule adequately, have misplaced priorities and manage themselves poorly with respect to time. The procrastination parasite thrives on these individuals. They are so busy hopping from one job to another and dealing with constant interruptions that they postpone everything that isn't yet a crisis.

If you are a victim of disorganization, act now. Have written goals. Plan your months, days and hours. Give priority to those tasks that will lead you closer to your goals. Make appointments with yourself to start each project at a particular time. And keep those appointments. Schedule those long or distasteful activities early in the day. Then get a head start by starting early. A fast and productive start sets the stage for a productive day. Practice self-discipline. Make up your mind that you are going to adopt a *do it now* attitude. For help in getting organized, refer to my book, *Making Time Work For You.* Meanwhile, here are ten suggestions for getting organized and gaining control of your time.

Put your goals in writing. Time is life. Don't leave

it to chance. Determine where you would like to be in ten years or five years and put those goals in writing. Then schedule time for yourself to work in that direction. Where you will be in ten years or five years is determined by what you are doing today, tomorrow and next week. If you don't have goals, you won't realize the full impact of procrastination.

Organize your work area. An organized desk is not the sign of a sick mind, it is the sign of an organized mind. People do better on exams when neatly dressed, excel in sales when well-prepared, and are more productive at work when their materials are arranged in an orderly way. Keep your in-basket off your desk to minimize interruptions and distractions. If possible, have your desk face the wall. Disorganization breeds procrastination.

Plan your day. If you have no objectives for the day you will likely have a matching set of results. Plans are the handrails that guide you through the day's distractions and keep you on course. Plan what you will do at the start, evaluate progress during the day, and measure results at the finish. Planning is the enemy of procrastination.

Schedule your tasks. Listing important jobs on a "to do" list shows your intention to work on them; but scheduling them in your planner reveals a commitment to get them done. Make appointments with yourself at specific times to work on your priority tasks. And try to keep those appointments. If you can continually commit yourself to work on planned tasks at predetermined times, you will defeat the tendency to procrastinate.

Handle paper only once. When possible, that is. Don't even look at your mail until you have 30 to 60 minutes available to review it. As you pick up each piece of paper, either scrap it, delegate it, do it, file it, or schedule a time to do it later. The same thing applies to e-mail. It's impossible to do it now and procrastinate at the same time.

Write it down. Writing things down does not mean you are circumventing your memory - you are simply helping it to do its job. We all need reminders to prevent a myriad of essential tasks from being delayed simply because they conveniently keep slipping our mind. The pen is mightier than the sword - and it writes better.

Say no more often. Some people say, *yes* to others simply because they're available or don't want to offend. Make sure the request is compatible with your goals before you agree. Have as much respect for your own time as you have for other peoples' time. Remember, every time you say *yes* to something, you are saying *no* to something else that could be more important. This is worse than procrastination because you will never have time to do the things that should be done.

Delegate more. This is the greatest time-saver of all; because it frees up time for more important tasks. If you have no one to delegate to, ask your suppliers to help. Don't delegate anything that can be eliminated. And don't delegate to procrastinators without having a fool-proof follow-up system.

Practice Pareto's Principle. This 80-20 rule suggests that 80% of your results are achieved by 20% of the things you do. Focus on the priorities, and if anything gets put off or doesn't get done, at least let it be the less important tasks.

Don't procrastinate. Procrastination is the nemesis of organization. Putting things off wastes time, causes stress and helps make life unpleasant for yourself and others. By practicing the nine suggestions above as well as the recommendations in this book, you will be able to gain control of your time and your life.

16 Perfectionism is procrastination's ally

Perfectionism is procrastination's ally

Aperfectionist is one who spends an inappropriate amount of time on a task. A perfectionist believes that *if a job is worth doing at all it is worth doing well.* Unfortunately the word *well* to a perfectionist means *perfect.* The result in many cases is that more time and effort is expended than the end result justifies. In other cases the job isn't even completed on time, if completed at all.

Many goals are never achieved simply because the individual waited for enough time to do a "good" job. Time is at a premium for everyone and "enough time" for a perfectionist is rarely available. Therefore perfectionism and procrastination frequently go hand in hand.

Recognize that every task has a point of diminishing return. Make up your mind in advance that you will only devote a certain amount of time to the job. For example, don't wash your car until it is so clean it squeaks; wash it as well as you can in the half hour you have allocated to that job. Let the time spent be in proportion to the importance of the task.

You cannot always conclude that a person is a perfectionist simply because he or she is spending a lot of time on a project and getting everything letter perfect. It depends on the value of the results. A public speaker might be perceived to be a perfectionist for arriving two hours early, testing the microphone, laying out all the materials, adjusting the overhead, screen, chairs, and perhaps even rehearsing the opening comments. But if the person's objective is to do a great job, earn credibility, win more contracts, and increase the bottom line, the results justify the extra time spent. Similarly, a real estate agent who researches the community he or she is farming, checks out recent sales, summarizes listings in the area comparable to the prospect's home, plans a presentation in detail, and spends hours reviewing details before making the contact, could be viewed as a perfectionist. But if the result is to get a listing and a fat commission check, the extra effort is warranted.

What usually differentiates a perfectionist from a planner is the value of the task being worked on. Usually about 20 percent of our activities produce 80 percent of our results. Identifying those 20 percent, and spending twice as much time on them as our competitors are spending, is not being a perfectionist, it's being smart.

But there are so many interesting and enjoyable activities among those 80 percent that only produce 20 percent of our results that we are frequently tempted to fall prey to perfectionism. The longer we spend on those unimportant, pleasant activities, the longer we can delay working on those meaningful goals we have set for ourselves. Having a neat, tidy desk with books in alphabetical order and a color-coded planner are sure pleasing to the eye. And they actually save time while you're working at your desk. But if 80 percent of your value is from personal contact with clients in the field, the hours being spent re-organizing books and files could legitimately be called both perfectionism and procrastination. Learn to operate with your objectives in mind. Spend the majority of your time on the key priorities that relate to those objectives. And if, in the process, your painting must remain at half-mast and your pencils in disrepair, so be it.

We should budget our time, spending more time on the goal-related priorities and less on the small stuff. If it's true that eighty percent of our results are from twenty percent of the things we do, it follows that if we were to concentrate the bulk of our time and effort on the twenty percent and do a mediocre job on the eighty percent, the results would be phenomenal. This does not mean we should do sloppy work eighty percent of the time. We should do the best we can in the time that we have allocated to that eighty percent. But the additional improvement we would get by attempting to do it perfectly would not justify the greater expenditure of time.

Perfectionists should ask themselves, "What would be the impact on the company or family or career if this project were submitted as it is?" If the answer were "Nothing," it would probably be counterproductive to spend more time refining it. Let the amount of time allocated be proportional to the value of the project. And spend time based on objectives, not feelings.

Whether perfectionism has stemmed from unrealistic expectations of parents or teachers, unrealistic demands of a boss, or whether it's a habit acquired from years of seeking approval and acceptance, it can be modified if we accept ourselves for who we are, evaluate our use of time, and strive to maintain balance in our lives.

17 Don't be afraid of fear

Don't be afraid of fear

Some people procrastinate because they're afraid of what might happen if they make a mistake. This is akin to perfectionism except that they are paralyzed by fear rather than by the need to do something perfectly. Thus they fail to get a medical check-up, not because it's inconvenient, but because they're afraid of what the results might be.

These people must acknowledge the fear and do it anyway. Although most of their fears are unfounded, they are fears, nonetheless. And we must have a burning desire to want to change or we will continue to be trapped by our own inertia.

Some people seem to have so many things to worry about nowadays. They get totally caught up in an emotion that not only wastes time and precipitates procrastination, but also damages their health. It could result in migraines, ulcers, burnout, emotional breakdown or worse.

Think back for a moment over the events of this past week. Then ask yourself a question: "How much time did I spend worrying?" Once you have the estimate, ask yourself another question: "What did my worrying accomplish?"

Nothing positive is ever accomplished through worry. *Concern* is a different matter. There's nothing wrong with being concerned when your son is an hour late getting home, or your car won't start, or you don't have enough money to pay the mortgage. Concern prompts you to take action to rectify the situation. Concern shows that you're human. Concern is justified. But a person who blows a real or imagined problem way out of proportion and allows it to control their thoughts to the point where they can never get it out of their mind, is not only concerned, he or she is *worried*.

If worry doesn't accomplish anything, how can we stop ourselves from worrying? The first thing we have to do is recognize that we tend to think the worst. Studies indicate that 40 percent of our worries are about things that never happen. Another 30 percent of our worries concern things that are in the past and we would be unable to do anything to change them anyway.

Twelve percent of our worries are needless concerns about our health, probably due to our overactive - and pessimistic - imaginations. Ten percent of our worries are petty, miscellaneous worries. Only eight percent of our worries are about real, legitimate concerns.

So put your problem into perspective. Recognize the fact that some of your fears could be unfounded. Which brings us to the suggestion mentioned in a previous chapter - think positively. Nothing is as defeating as a negative attitude. Sure, your son could be late because of a car accident. But he also could have run out of gas, or stopped for a pizza, or decided to drop in on a friend on the way home. A client may not have returned a telephone call because he's not interested in doing business with your firm anymore. But he also could have been called out of the office unexpectedly or be tied up in a meeting or have forgotten about the message. Whenever you're confronted with something of concern, immediately think of three or four positive possibilities. You might as well approach life with a positive attitude, since 92 percent of the worries are unnecessary anyway.

What if there's *nothing* positive about the situation? What if it's a definite disaster? In that case, worry is still futile. You must distinguish between what you can and cannot control. If there's something you can do to change the situation or prevent something from happening, do it. Don't procrastinate. Action dissipates worry. Alternatively, worry tends to debilitate us. It inhibits productive activity and drains our resource of energy. So take action immediately. If it's impossible to take action, if it's completely beyond your control, worry is still futile. Take solace in the fact that it's not the end of the world. Deal with today's problems today, but don't make it harder on yourself by taking on tomorrow's problems as well. Whatever you do, don't let worry fester inside you. Talk it out. Discuss it with a close friend or your boss. It's surprising how much lighter a burden becomes when you vocalize it.

18 Plan to say no

Plan to say no

If you fail to plan, your time will be spent working on other people's priorities instead of your own. People postpone activities that are important to them because of a reluctance to say *no*. It's understandable; it's so easy to say *yes*. But although we avoid the immediate pain of disappointing someone, we suffer a greater disappointment later because of an important job left unfinished.

When you plan, you determine what important tasks you would like to accomplish in the weeks and months ahead. Then you list the various steps (if more than one is required) in order to complete those tasks, and estimate the amount of time it would take to complete each step. To this you add a realistic safety factor to allow for interruptions, problems, etc., and schedule the total time in your planner.

Then, if someone asks if you're doing anything Friday night, a quick glance at your planner will prompt you to say, "Oh, I see we have a commitment that night. Why?" If anything has to be postponed, perhaps it should be the other person's request. It's easier to say *no* when a prior commitment has been made.

Many people waste time and accomplish little because of a lack of planning. Since TV networks plan their schedules well in advance, they know exactly what will be telecast Friday night. And if you don't have Friday night planned yourself, guess who loses by default?

Don't allow your calendar to fill up with other people's priorities while yours lie dormant on a wish list. Take charge of your own life by determining what you want to accomplish this month and this year. These are your goals. You will achieve them if you plan to achieve them. But planning is more than simply jotting them on a *to do* list; it is blocking off time in your planning calendar, making an appointment with yourself. You are then obliged to keep that appointment, just as you are obliged to keep an appointment with your client, doctor, or close friend.

This doesn't mean you never say *yes* to a request, but it does mean you should evaluate the request to determine whether it is more important than the activity you are planning to work on in that time period. If it *is* more important, perhaps you should let it displace your planned activity. But never postpone your own plans simply because they *can* be postponed. This is procrastination. Because of a reluctance to say no, many plans are never realized and goals remain unachieved.

Say *no* or *yes* solely on the basis of the importance of the request compared to the importance of your own planned activity. And make sure you *do* plan; for those who don't plan are at the mercy of those who do.

If you want to increase commitment and add the pressure of a deadline, schedule chunks of time in your planner in which to carry out the small segments of *overwhelming* tasks. These *appointments with yourself* ensure that your plans are not displaced by the demands of other people. If you want something to get done, schedule it to be done.

19 Fight procrastination with routines

Fight procrastination with routines

As mentioned earlier, many of the tasks we tend to put off are those that we simply don't like to do, whether it's returning phone calls, answering complaints making cold calls to prospects or writing that weekly report. One way of fighting this tendency is to schedule these tasks for the same time each day. Tasks performed again and again at the same time each day become a habit, like brushing your teeth or taking a shower. Few of us even think about whether routine activities like brushing our teeth are enjoyable or not. We simply *do* them. They are a necessary part of living, and take little time or effort.

For example, you could return telephone calls every day at 11 a.m. and 4 p.m., spend one hour each morning from 9 a.m. to 10 a.m. making cold calls and write letters first thing after lunch each day.

Allowing tasks to accumulate makes it easier to procrastinate. It's a lot more difficult to return ten calls than it is to return five of them. And it's a lot more time-consuming to write twenty letters than it is to respond to five of them. Procrastination breeds procrastination. Don't allow jobs to get ahead of you. Do them on a regular basis so they become a daily routine as opposed to a weekly adventure.

Be careful that these routines don't become ruts. Eventually someone will find a better way of doing almost everything. So periodically question what you are doing, why you are still doing it and how you are doing it. A routine is not something you do without thinking; it is something you do without procrastinating.

20 Working with procrastinators

Working with procrastinators

If you are not a procrastinator yourself, but have to work with them, there are a few things you can do besides pass along this book. First, you should empathize with them, even if you're annoyed. Procrastination is a common timewaster that affects almost everyone to some degree. Be patient, understanding and helpful. They are only doing what comes naturally. There is usually nothing vindictive or even intentional in their action, or more accurately, inaction.

Be firm, however, in your attempts to get them moving. Place deadlines on all requests and follow up at regular intervals. Be explicit in your instructions and obtain feedback so there is no chance of a misunderstanding. Emphasize the importance of completing the task on time and the reason it's important. If the individual is a member of your staff, make it clear that the ability to adhere to deadlines is one factor that is taken into consideration when evaluating performance.

Before giving an assignment to a procrastinator, anticipate the reasons that they may have for delaying the task. If they claim that it's a big job, tell them that's the reason that you are providing more time. Explain that if they start right away and do a little each day, they will have more than enough time. If they claim that they are too busy, be prepared to discuss the projects that they have on their plates, the priority of each, and how they could budget their time in order to complete them. Don't be too quick to offer help by assigning tasks to someone else or volunteering to do them yourself. If you make it too easy for them, it will *encourage* procrastination rather than prevent it. But recognize that they can't do everything at once and be prepared to reprioritize some of the other projects if necessary.

Look for signs that they lack confidence in themselves and offer encouragement. Bolster their egos by reminding them of some past accomplishment. Make your trust in their abilities obvious. Be quick to praise them for small successes as they work on their assignments.

Procrastinators need structure, so put instructions and expected completion dates in writing. Have a pre-determined series of reporting dates in place. Record these dates in your planner so you will be sure to follow up on schedule.

Don't overlook the possibility that they need on-the-job training and self-development courses. Time management, personal organization, goal-setting and project management training are particularly helpful to procrastinators. Assure them that you or others are available for guidance or advice. Let them know that they are not being left alone to sink or swim.

When evaluating their progress, don't compare them to others or to yourself. Determine whether there is any improvement compared to their past behavior. Everyone is unique and develops at different rates. The important thing is that they continue to improve their performance with time. Be sure to communicate this improvement to them; don't wait for the formal performance review to offer feedback and encouragement.

Finally, share with them some of the ideas contained in this book, including the advantages of doing distasteful tasks during their prime time, scheduling blocks of time in their planner to work on assignments and chipping away at large tasks a little at a time during spare moments.

Before you label anyone a procrastinator, make sure their delays are not merely isolated incidents beyond their control. Procrastination is the intentional and continual postponement of a task that should be done now. The odd postponement is neither unusual nor serious. And don't assign trivial or useless tasks that are better eliminated. As long as there are important tasks undone, the trivial tasks *should* be postponed.

21 Twenty-five ways to overcome procrastination

Twenty-five ways to overcome procrastination

The ideas summarized below should serve as assists in kicking the procrastination habit, regardless of its underlying cause. Choose those ideas that you feel comfortable using. All of them have been found helpful to some people.

➤ Set a goal for the thing you've been putting off. Pick a specific date to do it, and schedule time in your planner to get it done.

➤ List the advantages of doing the task and compare them with the consequences of not doing it. The result may convince you that it should be done.

➤ List the things you have been putting off, choose the simplest task and do it. This small success should motivate you to tackle other, more difficult tasks that you have been delaying.

➤ Decide on a reward for finishing a task that you have been delaying. Example: a coffee break, new dress, a night on the town. Provide yourself with an incentive to get it done.

➤ Break down the overwhelming tasks into chunks, and do them a little at a time.

➤ Schedule the task in your prime time when you are at your peak mentally and physically. For most people this is first thing in the morning.

➤ If the task you've been putting off is work-related, put the appropriate paperwork or other material on your desk when you go home so it alone will be visible when you arrive the next morning.

➤ Commit yourself to do the task at a definite time and tell others of your plans. Many of us will act to avoid embarrassment with our peers.

➤ Get help. Delegate some of the distasteful tasks, or share the task with others willing to help.

➤ Do absolutely nothing. Some people find they get bored and will tackle anything rather than remain idle.

➤ Place deadlines on all tasks that you have been putting off.

➤ Keep telling yourself, "If it's unpleasant, I'll do it now and get it over with."

➤ If you tend to be a perfectionist, recognize that good is good enough and that it's better to get it done than to delay until it can be perfect.

➤ If you're afraid of failing, acknowledge the fear and do it anyway. Recognize that successful people fail more because they try more.

➤ Disorganization breeds procrastination, so get organized.

➤ Tackle the distasteful tasks when you're on a high – when you have just accomplished something significant and feel good about yourself.

➤ Accept full responsibility for the task; don't allow excuses to lull you into procrastination.

➤ Engage in positive self-talk. Be optimistic. Attitude can make a difference.

➤ Force yourself to start. Once started, you'll build momentum. Keep starting, and you'll develop the *do it now* habit.

➤ Don't wait until you have more time; you will probably have no more time in the future than you have right now.

➤ If you don't feel like working on the task, do something small that will take you in the right direction. Getting started is the hardest part of doing.

➢ Recognize that you have a choice to either do something or not do it. Take full responsibility for how you spend your time.

➢ Don't put yourself on a guilt trip if you *do* procrastinate once in a while. It's okay not to be perfect.

Conclusion

Conclusion

You should not be embarrassed or ashamed if you procrastinate. Everybody does it at one time or another. It's a natural tendency. But you can increase your effectiveness tenfold if you are able to curb this tendency. To do this requires conscious effort on your part. But you *can* do it, either by sheer self-discipline or by practicing some of the techniques described in this book. In either case you must *want* to change. The more you want to change, the easier the process becomes. Motivation plays a big role in any behavioral change.

If you are a chronic procrastinator, i.e., you intentionally and habitually postpone tasks that should be done immediately, you will gain the most from reviewing this brief book and immediately applying some of its suggestions. Start with a task or activity whose delay has been causing some problems. Resolve now that you will never procrastinate on that job again. This not to say that you will not put off *other* tasks. But concentrate on never putting off that one selected task.

It's important that you don't try to stop procrastinating on *everything*. This in itself would be an overwhelming assignment doomed to failure. Tackle your problem a bite at a time, one job at a time. When you are confident that you no longer procrastinate on that job, pick another one and direct your energies there. Procrastination is defeated a job at a time. Each small success is motivational and will make your next resolve easier.

Don't be discouraged if you slip once in a while. Developing the *do it now* habit is a process, not an event. Each time you succeed, the process becomes a little easier. Success breeds success.

Congratulations on taking the first step in a process that will help you stop procrastinating and gain control of your life.

A note from the author

I would love to hear from you. What worked best for you? Were you successful by using a technique not mentioned in this book? Have you had an experience where procrastination has had a significant impact on your life? Share your experiences and I will try to incorporate them into a revised edition of this book. Electronic format is preferred, so please e-mail your comments to Harold@TaylorOnTime.com. Or mail them to the address appearing elsewhere in this book.

Harold Taylor
November, 1999

Other books on procrastination

Barnes, Joseph, E. *Super Pro-crastinators.* New York: Barnes Books, 1985.

Bliss, Edwin. *Doing It Now: A 12-Step Program for Curing Procrastination & Achieving Your Goals.* New York: Charles Scribner's Sons, 1983.

Broadus, Loren. *How to Stop Procrastinating and Start Living.* Minneapolis, MN: Augsburg Publishing House, 1983.

Burka, Jane B. and Lenora M. Yuen. *Procrastination.* Reading, MA: Addison-Wesley, 1983.

Ellis, Albert and William J. Knaus. *Overcoming Procrastination.* New York: New American Library, 1977.

Lively, Lynn. *The Procrastinator's Guide to Success.* New York: McGraw-Hill, 1999.

Pollar, Odette. *50 Ways to Conquer Procrastination.* Oakland, CA: Time Management Systems, 1993.

Porat, Frieda. *Creative Procrastination.* New York: Harper & Row Publishers, 1980.

Roberts, M. Susan. *Living Without Procrastination.* Oakland, CA: New Harbinger Publications, 1995.

Sapadin, Dr. Linda. *It's About Time!: The 6 Styles of Procrastination and How to Overcome Them.* New York: Penguin, 1996.

Sherman, James R. *Stop Procrastinating. Do it!* Golden Valley, MN: Pathway Books, 1983.

Index

For a free catalog of time management books, products and training instruments, contact:

Harold Taylor Time Consultants Inc.
2175 Sheppard Ave. E., Suite 310
North York, Ontario, Canada M2J 1W8
Telephone: 416-491-0777; Fax 416-491-8233
Web site: www.TaylorOnTime.com
Harold@TaylorOnTime.com